To

Leonard Rees Esq.

who has made even Sunday

enjoyable.

From

William Watson

Nov 5, 1925

Poems Brief and New

POEMS
BRIEF AND NEW

BY
SIR WILLIAM WATSON

LONDON
JONATHAN CAPE LTD

FIRST PUBLISHED IN MCMXXV
MADE & PRINTED IN GREAT BRITAIN
BY BUTLER & TANNER LTD
FROME AND
LONDON

Contents

5

Prefatory Note

EXCEPTING such fairly numerous pieces as all we men of rhyme habitually write and destroy, this little volume comprises everything that I have done in verse during these very latest years. Its contents, for the most part, now make their first appearance in print, almost the only exceptions being the two little poems entitled 'No Surrender!' and 'The Mother of Doom,' which were contributed to *The Times* during certain critical moments in Great Britain's domestic affairs. I reprint them here, not because I am under any delusions as to their literary importance, which is obviously *nil*, but because I think that a poet owes it to himself not to hide or suppress what he has once honestly written concerning aught that touches his country's welfare.

There is perhaps no real occasion for me to say anything further; but as regards those contents of this book which are more typical of it than its very few lines on national or public matters, I will go so far as to remark that in all, or nearly all, of these poems and verses I have studied *brevity*; that quality which Sir Joshua Reynolds, in words recalling much older ones, accuses Bacon of studying to excess,[1] and which I could wish that some of our poets, from Spenser's day onwards, had studied more. Unfortunately, it is one of those virtues which, as a rule, must be their own reward, for many readers undoubtedly admire concentration less than expansion, and seem hardly to suspect how vastly easier is the second than the first.

Just another word. In the course of these pages, though quite aside from their main current, are two or three pieces of a satirical nature. In the longest of them, while some present-day literary tendencies are undisguisedly assailed, no living individual writer is alluded to.

W. W.

[1] 'But he studies brevity to excess; and therefore his meaning is sometimes doubtful.'—*Sir Joshua Reynolds to the students of the Royal Academy, Dec.* 14, 1770.

The Marble Fountain

IN calm and tempest, in shine and shade,
On a faultless emerald lawn,
A marble fountain for ever played,
From dawn unto conquering dawn.

No rainbow'd bliss had the fountain lacked,
And its gaiety nought could mar,
Till it heard the Voice of the Cataract
In an Alpine gorge afar.

'With thunder of battle, in glory and gloom,
I have torn,' said the torrent, 'my way.'
And the fountain murmured, 'My cruel doom
Is to play — and play — and play.'

The Storms and the Havens

YOUR eyes were pining southward, and you
    said, 'The lands are yonder
    That can woo me with sweet fierceness o'er the
        interloping sea.'
But I answered, 'Oh, I care not whether south or
    north we wander,
    For the world is lovely everywhere if roam'd
        through with thee.'

We lingered by the waters as they rose and
    subsided;
    We watched the plumy children of the foam
        and the spray;
We saw the massing clouds that in a moody silence
    glided;
    We heard the tempest peal, amid the ruins of
        the day.

And the Ocean to this land of ours a wild kiss was
    throwing,
    From the lips that ever babble of the Far and
        Unknown;
And the dream-tides were lapping, and the dream-
    winds blowing,
    In the harbours that we voyage to with dream-
        sails alone.

The Lark and the Thrush

O FROM too far, and from too high,
   In too pure air above,
Doth the great Rhapsodist of the Sky
   Utter melodious love.

Bird that from neighbouring tree dost pour
   Songs of less heavenly birth,
'Tis thine, thine, that can pierce me more,
   Sweet Rhapsodist of the Earth.

The Visitor Abhorred

UNKNOWABLE Power is o'er me —
The might of unknowable Mind;
And fathomless Time is before me,
And fathomless Time is behind.

And I sit at the Feast of Illusion
In the Palace of Baffled Quest,
Awaiting the loathed intrusion .
Of the silent Unbidden Guest,

Who passes the sleeping sentry,
And leaves him to slumber on —
And makes his triumphal entry,
And casts his dart, and is gone.

The Necessity of Wrath

GREAT and far Star, built yonder in gloom,
Art thou as tranquil as men might conceive
    thee,
Mortals accurst with immortal desire?
Nay, in thy bosom no peace may bloom;
Passions convulse thee, rages upheave thee,
Thy birth was fury, thy life is fire,
Thou art oceans of violence, abysses of ire,
And dreadfullest Calm shall but signal thy doom,
When the wealth of thy fierceness for ever shall
    leave thee,
And all that is Thou shall in ashes expire.

The Tomb of the Mighty

DISTURB not — thou wilt find him unfor-
giving —
   The great and famed, in his sepulchral bed!
Thou mayst out-tire the malice of the living,
   But not the vengeance of the implacable dead.

The Enamoured Lute

A SWEET lute pined in a palace,
And heard the slow years roll,
And it dreamed of the mighty musician,
Who alone drew forth its soul.

It abode mid splendour and glory,
Mid stately and gracious things,
But afar were the magic fingers,
Beloved of the magic strings.

And the great sun looked on its pining,
And the calm moon gazed on its pain,
And they left it to dream of its hero
And be wooed by the world in vain.

The Thrallers and the Thrall

THE Gods, being merry, and having for a
   whim
Created Man to make a jest of him,
And taken counsel of their hearts how best
To crown with a pure perfectness the jest,
Set him fast-anchored shiplike mid the foam
Of the Infinite Seas he else had joyed to roam.

There doth he bear, while tempest round him
   flits,
The laughter of the great, high, heavenly Wits;
And there, though he persuades himself that he
Is well contented with captivity,
He dreams of the isles he never hath espied,
And the far oceans to his sails denied.

The Faithless and the Constant

THOU who at will canst fling
  Thine insolent alms or bid me pine de-
    frauded, —
Compared to Sorrow thou'rt a shallow thing,
Joy, the much lauded.

Ah, with pale promise, thou
Awhile perhaps mayst hoodwink and deceive me,
But it is Sorrow that hath kept her vow
Not once to leave me.

The Desert Heart

I HATE the cold, void, desert heart,
That feels no human pain
When to their doom fair things depart,
  To charm not Earth again.

Heart out of husks and offal made,
  Thy presence will suffice
To cast o'er Hell a drearier shade,
  Or poison Paradise.

Earthworship

ALL vast, vague dreams, as things of little
worth,
   Contentedly I leave to dreamful men;
And without murmur live the life of Earth —
   The only world I ken:

A world perhaps as fair as the orbs above,
   That took with such a flaunted unconcern
My adoration, and the midnight love
   That asked for no return!

Brightly, O Earth, they rest or roam in Space,
   But thou for ever unto me art more, —
Sweet-breathing Mother of a bitter race
   That vaunts its unsweet lore.

Baffled Deity

GOD hath His failures, nowise few. Behind
His mighty dreams the oft-foiled Dreamer
   lurks,
The aroma of perfection round His mind
Reaching not half His works;
And thus doth the Idealist of the Spheres,
The Great Arch-Visionary, at moments wear
Delight that seems first cousin to despair
On His lone countenance void of mirth and tears!
For He is everywhere
The Eternal Master planning without cease
The Eternal Masterpiece —
Alas, impossibly fair.

Give Not to Me

GIVE not to me, mid the thunder
  And speed of the world's hot wheels,
Such love as perhaps the Marble
  For the Alabaster feels.

But love me with love as fiery
  As the furnace whence arose
Both Marble and Alabaster,
  In the Earth's primeval throes.

A Word with Fortune

I NEVER ask to live and bask
  In sunlight splendid.
I take my share of foul and fair
  Till life be ended.

When knaves prevail I do not wail
  And rend my raiment.
I bide the day when haply they
  Shall reap due payment.

I nurse no spleen 'gainst Powers unseen,
  Ev'n if they leave me
Torn to and fro 'twixt bliss and woe
  Till Earth receive me.

O Shall my Soul

O SHALL my soul crave only bliss —
Her that is captured, when throngs are chas-
ing,
By none but him who never pursues?
O shall I pine, mad for her kiss,
Withered and parched in a dream of embracing
Her who may change into mists and dews?

Give me the toils, give me the tears,
Give me the pangs of greatness and glory,
Not their delight or power alone!
Nay, mid the darts — nay, mid the spears, —
Leave me encoiled with the stars and their story,
Till to their silence I bring mine own.

The Unvanquished

MY heart's companion, let
Us two forget,
And so make vain, all rude
Vicissitude,
And Time's betrayals, and countermine them yet!

Ah, Fortune's ebb we know,
More than her flow;
But not soon conquered, we
Hazard her sea,
And with much laughter through the gales we go.

Nature's Indiscretions

NATURE, uncircumspect, oft talks to Man,
  And frankly tells him everything she can.
For her proud dowry is immortal youth,
And all the young blurt out at times the truth.

The Songsters

SING, Nightingale! There still be those who take
  Thy music to be sweet.
Chant thine old chant — till the new fashions make
  All melody obsolete.

I cannot doubt that soon the corncrake's note
  Shall be to thine preferred!
What then? Sing on, — with thy still golden throat,
  Still tolerated bird!

The Elf-King's Daughter

THE Kingdom of Elfland, proud and free,
  With only the Law of Delight to bind it,
Where is it truly famed to be?
  'Tis wheresoever we list to find it.

O'erwatched by all its peaks of gold,
  There dwelt beside the Magic Water,
In forests drowsy with silence old,
  That wild white Bliss, the Elf-King's Daughter.

And the elfin world was all she knew,
  Till at last, on rash and luckless pinions,
Out of her father's realm she flew,
  And sped across Night to Man's dominions.

She flew through calms, she flew through storms,
  She alighted here and mocked at danger;
But soon she beheld two darksome forms —
  Pain the Unknown, and Death the Stranger.

Aghast she gazed upon both these twain:
  She had seen no shapes that theirs resembled.
No word had she heard of Death or Pain,
  And they looked in her face and she quailed
    and trembled.

She strove to flee, upon mistlike wings,
    But the mistlike wings, with foiled endeavour,
Drooped at her sides as useless things,
    Palsied in this our air for ever.

So here she remains, a wandering sprite,
    And guards her secret and veils her story;
And sometimes, far in the heart of night,
    She hath a glimpse of her vanished glory.

For then this region in dreams she spurns,
    Revisits the verge of the Magic Water,
In dreams to her father's court returns,
    And is — till the dawn — the Elf-King's
        Daughter.

November, 1921

Cease, Foolish Rosebud

CEASE, foolish rosebud, cease unfolding
So fast thy bosom's guarded sweetness!
Thy charm was a most rich withholding;
  Thy beauty, a perfect incompleteness.

Ah, by thy youth to-day enchanted,
  I must endure a honied sorrow,
Finding thy lovely self supplanted
  By thy yet lovelier self to-morrow.

A Half-real Solace

THOUGH I may sink o'erborne at last
In suddenness of the felling blast,
This do I know: when life is past,
Not quite shall I be out of place
In the earnest fire-fierce Earth's embrace,
As less a man than a grimace.

Rather shall I be wholly at home,
'Mid the still quick and flameful loam.

The Two Ifs

IF joy be thine, then guard the boon
From the gazing sun and the prying moon!
In a world that is lean with dearth of bliss,
'Twere cruel to flaunt a gift like this.

And if thine be woe, then do thy best
To immure it deep in thy cloistering breast!
'Twere callous to blazon abroad thy pain,
And harrow some happier heart in vain.

The Gamesters

MUSIC and Poesy, like Gods at play,
Diced for the domination of my soul.
Poesy won, — yet oft, too easy in sway,
Lets Music snatch control.

In a Library

THE bard of Power, — the bard of Grace, —
 Which shall be chief? Nay, why inquire?
Here they have proud but equal place
 In the great peerage of the lyre.

To him who sumptuous wine adores,
 No sovereign vintage comes amiss:
With the same reverence, he outpours
 The ruddy or the golden bliss.

The Terrors of Truth

A MIGHTY wizard gave to an eastern King
The power to see, for but a single day,
Through all disguise, beholding everything
　　Stript bare of false array.

Then, to the monarch's gaze made manifest
　　In their true lineaments and native forms,
Foul demons, at the Enchanter's dread behest,
　　Came and passed by in swarms.

Yonder was that which he had deemed to be
　　Fair-smiling Friendship – one gorgonian frown;
And yonder was self-named Fidelity,
　　Plotting to seize his crown.

And hour by hour, serene and grave and mute,
　　He looked on the nude souls of evil things,
With the great calm that is the attribute
　　Of god-descended Kings.

But prone he fell, being heart-cleft, when he saw
　　At last revealed, in light not from above,
Solely the harpy Beak, the harpy Maw,
　　Known, to the crowned, as Love.

The Exiles

LOOK, – the New Rose is rich and fair.
She puts imperial raiment on.
She hath the large imperial air;
  But whither is the perfume gone?

Banished afar, it fled on wings
  That bore it hence in haste unmeet,
With all the other cast-out things
  That kept life sweet.

The Wizard's Crux

IF I, by wondrous fate, possessed
The all-transmuting Alkahest,
Famed to resolve the World's Contents
Into their mother elements,
I then might change thee by its powers
Back to the ingredients of the flowers!
But ah, what sovereign sorcery could
Witch them again to Womanhood?

O to Sail

O TO sail with thee, my dear,
Under headlands high and sheer,
At the mellow hour of daydroop when the lull of
  eve is near!

O to sail away, and be
From the curse of care set free,
Far from heart-ache, far from heart-break, on the
  great heart-healing sea.

Midnight

ONCE vainglorious, now forlorn:
  Dead and unlamented Year!
Thou to thy catafalque art borne,
  Without the escort of a tear.

Thine were hopes that lived unblest,
  Dying with the Summer's bloom.
They shall bestrew thy place of rest —
  The only flowers upon thy tomb.

Just a Possibility

I'LL take Life's hazards, rue not hours well
wasted,
  Hide my heart's wounds, ask no miraculous
    balm;
And ere I die, perhaps I shall have tasted
  At last a little calm.

I Care Not

I CARE not though the Spring forget
  Her golden promise made
To all the hearts that trust her yet,
  However oft betrayed.
I care not though the Moon above
  Forget the vassal Sea,
If thou, my love — if thou, my love —
  If thou forget not me.

I care not though in shadowy bower,
  With richest ruin strewn,
The Rose forget the entrancing hour
  Of her sweet tryst with June.
I care not though yon prideful grove
  Forget the stricken tree,
If thou, my love — if thou, my love —
  If thou forget not me.

The stars forget their ancient birth;
  The Sun forgets that time
When he espoused the youthful Earth
  In his commanding prime.
But far from where we mortals move,
  There shall some record be,
That I, my love — that I, my love —
  That I forgot not thee.

Dusk

THE bats are busy in moonless eve
   With the goblin web they seem to weave,
Here where the thrush, when morn was high,
Published his heart to the passer-by.

Twice, o'er the lane, like a guilty thing,
The shy owl flitted with noiseless wing,
Mid the silent breathing of frond and tree,
And of all that debauched the noontide bee.

Behind the fir-wood, red and large,
The sun went down like a warrior's targe;
And full of news from a secret shore,
The wanderer, Night, comes to the door.

The Forest Voices

I HEARD in the woodland a sound
From the heart of each visible thing;
And asking the reason, I found
   'Twas the Earth giving thanks for Spring.

The Youth of the World had returned,
   And the days were a Song of Re-birth,
Till I heard a great sighing, and learned
   'Twas Spring taking leave of the Earth.

Thy Passionate Breast

THY passionate breast, thy ruthful brow
    Thine eyes, the sisters of the sea —
Thy form and countenance — are they thou?
    Nay, but the fair, fit home of thee.

O head and neck like flower and stem,
    O sweeter voice than any bird's —
Lovely the bezel of the gem,
    Lovelier the jewel it engirds.

Thy Heart is Mine

CLEOPATRA, long ago, from cups of gold,
  Drank the molten pearls of Asia in her wine,
But my wealth is more than hers a hundredfold,
  For thy heart, for thy heart is mine.

Lofty Kings to whom the world did bow the knee,
  Lovely Queens that from afar in story shine,
They were all exceeding poor compared to me,
  For thy heart, for thy heart is mine.

Sonnet Written among the English Mountains

OFT, in reposeless youth, did I ascend
Yon heights of stormy peace, and gazing
down
Saw vales that affably take their own renown
With a frank gusto; chasms where cataracts rend
Silence in shards; and old grey roads that wend,
Circuitously as Fate, to an old grey town.
Thoughts of these things not time or tears may
drown,
And *one* thought shall rebuke me to the end.
For when the heavens, o'er deep-lulled valleys
green,
In splendid darkness burn, then do I rue,
That never from a great peak have I seen
The marshalled stars; never, beyond man's
view,
Lingered to watch, from lone-reared summit
serene,
Night sweeping past with all his retinue.

The Fowls of the Air

IN thickets and copses and hedges
The land-birds choose them a home,
But high on the wild cliff ledges
  Are the grey-winged folk of the foam.

Not theirs such voices as twitter
  And sing to the loved in the nest,
For the heart of the Ocean is bitter,
  And he drives all Song from his breast.

Yet dear are the crags of granite,
  And sweet is the smell of the sea,
To the Crested Grebe and the Gannet,
  And the mate of my soul, and me.

No Surrender!

VERSES WRITTEN AT A TIME OF INDUSTRIAL
CRISIS.

STAND fast at last, O weary Nation,
'Gainst inward foes that plot thy fall!
Stand firm – for that way lies salvation,
   And no way else at all.

Or yield – and be yet harder smitten!
   Yield – and then find 'twas worse than vain!
Yield – and still yield; and in fair Britain
   Let some foul Lenin reign.

Nay, yield no more, O weary Nation,
   Weary, but proud and mighty still!
In thine own hands is thy salvation,
   Thy Fate in thine own will.

The Mother of Doom

STRONG Tower of State, that unto rich and
poor,
In war and in scarce lovelier peace, hast been
Shelter and home: thou stood'st impregnable,
When willing toil and never-drowsing watch
Could guard thee from all access of decay.
But if dread Sloth, the mother of Doom, steal in,
And reign where Labour served, then is the hour
Hitherward posting, when men's eyes shall see
The thistle with the nettle strive for place
Within thy doorway, and men's ears shall hear
The owl hoot from a remnant of thy walls.

The False Summer

THE Summer that begrudged its honey,
  And promised boons it never gave,
Now, in its lean, mean parsimony,
  Departs unto its dirgeless grave.

Come, honest Winter! Thou at least
  Wilt not thy lack of heart conceal,
Or bid me to a monarch's feast
  To mock me with a beggar's meal.

January Down West

THE snowdrops are awake, in the Gateway of
the Year:
Already is the season of the daffodils near.
But the old trees shudder, the infirm trees fear,
For the storm comes rushing through the Gate-
way of the Year.

Oh, Spring has early spies, and in secret they are
here;
And Winter watches well, lest his enemies appear.
And Time looks backward with a misty eye and
blear,
And Love looks forward through the Gateway of
the Year.

To One in His Grave

YOU jested, smiled, and struck your wanton
　　blow:
　Take, mid the dead, this pardon from the
　　living.
For here on earth 'tis not the injured, — no,
　It is the injurers who are unforgiving.

Rejuvenescence

THE Day is young, the Day is sweet,
And light is her heart as the tread of her feet.

The Day is weary, the Day is old:
She has sunk into sleep through a tempest of gold.

Sleep, tired Day! Thou shalt rise made new,
All splendour and wonder and odour and dew.

The Thwarted Flower

WHERE none came near it the whole day
      long,
   It dwelt and bemoaned its lot —
The Flower whose name is itself a song,
   The divine Forget-me-not.

For its dream had been to live and die,
   Not desolate and unblest,
But close to the snowdrifts that belie
   The flame in a maiden's breast.

The Cosmic Lovers

DREAR as a laugh without mirth,
　Drear as a feast without wine,
Is the lorn, inconsolable Earth
　When the Sun will not shine.

Come forth and upraise her and cheer,
　And admit her, O Sun, to thy bliss!
For thou art her King without peer,
　And she lives for thy kiss.

The Noblest Victory

LOVE, the defier, and Time, the defied,
Wrestled for sway, being equals in pride ;
Love with his arrows about him as now;
Time with the dust of the stars on his brow.

Fate, intervening, gave rightful award:
'Time shall be vassal and Love shall be lord.'
And thus at her bidding they ended their feud,
Love, the subduer, and Time, the subdued.

Caprices of the Gods

UNSEASONABLE July,
   Pettish and rude and bleak —
Thou'rt Summer to the eye,
   But Winter to the cheek.

Was Nature wise to vary
   The order we held dear,
Turn revolutionary,
   And bolshevize the year?

Then let her sing and play
   Her carmagnolish tune —
But will December pay
   The debts of bankrupt June?

No, — 'twould yet more dishevel
   And tangle the wild dance,
The inebrious mazeful revel
   Of Nature's mad finance.

The Robe of Themis

HOW Justice in her courts may best be clothed
  Moves me not much or hotly;
But there's one garb that I have ever loathed –
  Ermine set off with motley.

On One of the Portraits of Emma, Lady Hamilton

SWEET witch, whose form and face do here
Make neighbouring loveliness appear
A thing most faulty, a thing most flaw'd,
Though once becrowned with fame and laud:
The mighty victor's victress, thou
Hast vanquished many heroes now,
And still triumphant, thou dost live
The great charm'd life that Art can give, —
Thy frailties past, — thy beauty alone
Less fragile than yon column'd stone.

Utopia

A LIFE too great for folly,
  In a world too wise for wine,
Is a life the saint or sage may love,
  But I cannot boast it mine.

If all by law were sober,
  And all by statute good,
I could not breathe the impeccable air —
  And I would not if I could.

No, if denied for ever
  All juice of grape or grain,
I'd leave this world to be destroyed
  By water once again.

To a Former 'Flame'

OFT is Fate in very truth
   Most benign when most severe!
Thou didst reject me in my youth:
   Ah, bitter day — ah, desperate year!
Once again we met of late —
And I am reconciled to Fate.

To a Young American Lady

WHO HAD WRITTEN TO ASK ME FOR MY BOOK-
PLATE

BOOKPLATE? I never had one. And my shelves
Carry no ruthless burden of books themselves.
Into a book called Life I oftener dip,
But even there I find a deal to skip:
Parts without glow — lack-lustre passages —
Its many soulless leaves — and round all these
The nightmare riddle of its authorship.

All Whom it may Concern

SINCE I remain a target still
For sundry valiant bowmen,
Here's to their health! I wish no ill
To honest, open foemen.

The shafts they fledge have never yet
Struck through to bone and marrow!
So I forgive — perhaps forget —
The archer and the arrow.

The Only Test

I'VE lived into a different day,
And watched the old day flee.
The men I know not arrive each hour;
  The men who know not me.
Their world or mine will perish,
  But which of them may it be?
Have patience. In less than a hundred years
  'Tis like enough thou'lt see.

To a Publicist and Sage

YOU that have found all Being a blaze of
   clearness:
  You that with loves and hates in blest control,
On the sleek lawns of life ignore the nearness
   Of the unextinct volcano of man's soul:

Pure, almost to eradicating gender:
  Somewhere in vales of innocence nursed apart:
Tempering our Night with your large spirit's
   splendour,
  And full of fire as a tomato's heart:

Still be yourself; still touch with tip of finger
  The daunting themes Thought pales at, from
   its birth;
And never ev'n for one rash moment linger
  Anywhere near the roots of aught on earth.

Go your chaste way, far though it be from *my* way;
  Take your rewards, and have your heart's
   desire;
But richer is the beggar on the highway
  Who once has sighted Truth, though from the
   mire.

A Recipe

THE method is simple. With care and with
    pains,
Conceal, if you have them, all semblance of brains.
Exclude from the scope and wide range of your pen
Whatever is still of some moment to men,
And prance on the memory of aught that has long
Been supposed, by a doddering world, to be Song.
Let Metre eternally jump, jolt, and lurch:
For infinite crudeness make infinite search.
Tradition — Form — fiddlesticks! Play your own
    part,
Like nothing in Nature — and nothing in Art.
But *if* you must needs follow *something*, then shun
Such bards as were lucid and large like the sun,
And always, as pattern and paradigm, take
The stagger of Donne or the stammer of Blake, —
Their few fine atonements for lame-footed speech
Being things rather palpably out of your reach.
Remember, a *spavinless* Pegasus counts,
In the eyes of true moderns, as poorest of mounts,
And nought that your fathers so blindly enjoyed
Can be else than a blunder their sons must avoid;
So beware lest a line inadvertently scan,

And of course be as odd and as queer as you can.
At the slightest intrusion of Grace take alarm,
And nip in the bud the least menace of Charm.
Let Euphony rank as a cardinal sin;
Be careful that Comeliness does not creep in;
And write in a fashion that makes men of sense,
At the mere name of Poetry, haste to fly hence.

But lose not an hour, lest the floodtide be past,
And the market for twaddle be glutted at last.

Statesmanship

WHEN I was young and rash, and dared
to feel
Anger at seeing the mighty o'erwhelm the weak,
And even called on mine own countrymen
To stay the trampler in his wildbeast rage;
Then did the Prudent and the Experienced lift
Rebuking hands, and councillors said: 'Young
man,
These matters are beyond thine understanding;
Leave them to minds nursed in the lore of State.'

The masters of that lore have had their way,
And shaped the course of our hurt world; and oft
I wonder if the foolishest of poets,
In his unwisdom, could have shaped it worse.

The Great and the Mean

FEAR not the wrath of deities. If they slay,
'Tis in a splendid and Olympian way.
Fear rather the quite earthly spleen of men;
And specially do thou fear,
Not a celestial spear,
But a most mortal pen.
It cannot, with Apollo's terrible grace,
Pierce and transfix thee in the market-place,
But it can do far worse! From year to year,
Unslaked, unsleeping, it can scratch thy face.

Destruction

THE grey walls, that in ruin here
    Moulder so darkly grand,
Perhaps did less august appear
    When perfect they did stand.

Time, take my thanks! Though fall'n do lie
    These towers beneath thy blows,
Yet doth thy rage but dignify
    The fabric it o'erthrows.

To a Government

YES, we are mighty: yet such things have been
　　As the imperceptible exit of proud Power,
When in a Nation whoso watched hath seen
　　Lax guardship of her dower.

Lords of Unthrift, it is of little use
　　To caulk and solder tiny leaks to-day,
If half our substance through your open sluice
　　Be madly drained away.

Look, – the lorn exile, fair Prosperity,
　　To happier lands returning, shuns these shores,
Where men undrowsed ask to what vast Dead Sea
　　Million on million pours.

No miser's heart hath England, but good will
　　Smiles not its best at thought of treasure spent
On limitless armies of the desk and quill
　　In boundless lavishment.

Lock, lock the floodgates! Ay, and act with speed,
　　For Fate, when mortals dally, comes in haste,
And loftiest, noblest wasters may indeed
　　Be then cast forth as waste.

The Wasps

I STEPT among wasps and hornets,
 And they rose like an angry cloud.
Their voices are shriller than cornets,
 And some of them thrice as loud.

Around me uncannily winging,
 And wheeling from heel to head,
They imagine persistent stinging
 Is bound to sting me dead.

For the wasp and his kin surpass us
 In patience immense and dire!
And the hornets around Parnassus
 No power on earth can tire.

They nurse their malevolence dreary,
 Yet find me surviving still;
For they are not harder to weary
 Than I am hard to kill.

The Easiest Revenge

IF one who lacks no just acclaim, and who
Stands like a living simile of success,
Should yet have sought to pierce me through and
    through
With his renowned pen-poniard, o'er and o'er,
Should I forgive him? Yes!
Nothing would cost me less,
Or gall *him* more.

A Wise Precaution

WHEN So-and-so gave us his 'Songs Without Flaws,'
It was What's-his-name managed the burst of
applause.

The strings of the lyre may at moments be 'struck,'
But, bless you, it's *pulling them* seems to bring luck.

The Pools of Evil

THE pathway that goes down unto perdition
Steeper and steeper at every stage of doom,
Doth at the last become a precipice sheer;
And where are they who journeyed to its verge
Merely as the explorers of strange lands,
With eye of quest and footstep of adventure
Seeking to gaze into the Pools of Evil
That simmer like enormous vats below?

Coolly, from that foul sight – as may beseem
Dispassionate students of putridity
And curious connoisseurs of festering life –
Some do indeed return, and bear thenceforward
No mark of sulliage graven on the soul.
But wouldst thou find *the others*, drag the pools.

The Stars in their Courses

ON the Ocean of Nought, where never a wave
is,
  There, through the vasts of silence lighted,
Ride the ten thousand heavenly navies,
  Under one High Command united.

With course unchanging, with speed unfailing,
  Amid their squadrons that know not slumber,
The duteous Earth, as of old, is sailing,
  With tackle and gear, with coil and cumber.

Who hath commanded her never to tarry?
  And out of what hidden, unguessed habitation
Beholds He the souls her decks do carry
  In endless voyage about Creation?

Cross Brow, Ambleside

MY smallest daughter had wondered how
Her dear home came by its name, Cross
Brow:[1]
Her home 'mid the meres, that loveliest seem
In their autumn trance and their winter dream:
Her home at the feet of the mountains high,
That have entanglements with the sky.

So I told her how, in a time half known
And half forgotten, a Cross of Stone,
Betwixt field and fellside, here had stood —
More frail than a certain Cross of Wood;
And how sweet souls that fared this way
May have halted before it to kneel and pray.

It is seen no longer, from dale or hill:
'Tis the Cross of Wood that is lasting still!
But here, in a world of pain and loss,
Where each must carry his destined cross,
A frolicsome child remembers now
Why the house she romps in is called Cross Brow,
Though little indeed Life's gleeful morn
Can know of the Brow that was crowned with
thorn.

1921.

[1] The author's dwelling at the time referred to.

The Saviours

YOU famed ones of old, who strove to guide,
   Justly and nobly, peoples and nations,
     In pathways high, where the high thoughts
     flower:
Though now, peradventure, ensphered you abide,
   Hardly beholding the Earth's tribulations,
     Lend us your wisdom for one great hour!

Nay, you are Shades! Past death and birth,
   Silent you dwell, in folds of the ages,
     Far from our wars and tears withdrawn,
While living hearts, on the living Earth,
   Dream there shall rise other heroes and sages
     Out of Creation's eternal dawn.

They shall rise – and haply shall rise in vain,
   On thankless mortals their greatness wasting,
     And, mighty of spirit, shall go to their doom;
Perhaps in the hour of the welter and pain
   Of a world to its final twilight hasting,
     Through fallen splendour and ruined bloom.

The Three Kinds of Song

SONG have I known that fed the soul,
And Song that was liker a foaming bowl;
But the Song that I account divine
Is at once rare food and noble wine.

Youth and the Muse

NO poet of golden name do I remember,
Who, when his youth was past, *began* to sing.
The blackbird cannot wait until September!
  Come peace, come war, his songs *will* out in
  Spring.

A Doubtful Necessity

I HAVE no use for verse as rough
As the acrid east's morose rebuff!
Even *without* such tuneless stuff
The world were dissonant enough.

An Impossible Novelty

THERE are, in Painting, Sculpture, Song,
  A few new ways of being wrong;
But it is plain to most men's sight
There's no new way of being right.

On a Politician

WHY call him fickle?   Two Constancies
    there be.
  Not *this* the faith to earth-firm anchorage pinned.
But then, in no less pure fidelity
  The Weathervane is anchored to the Wind.

Epitaph on an Obscure Person

STRANGER, these ashes were a Man
Crushed with a grievous weight.
He had acquired more ignorance than
He could assimilate.

Epitaph on a Famous Poet

MOURN, ye Parnassian singing-birds,
This singer, once your pride!
He lived with words — he lived *in* words —
He lived *for* words — and died.